UNDERSTANDING RELIGIONS

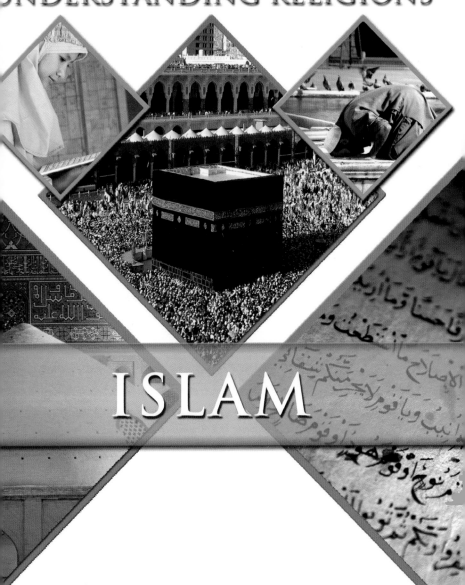

ISLAM

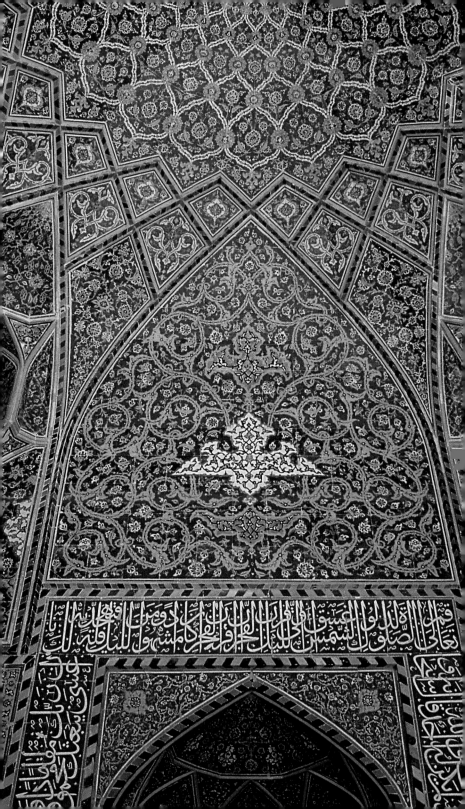

UNDERSTANDING RELIGIONS

ISLAM

MATTHEW S. GORDON

ROSEN
PUBLISHING®

New York

This edition published in 2010 by:

The Rosen Publishing Group, Inc.
29 East 21st Street
New York, NY 10010

Additional end matter copyright © 2010 by The Rosen Publishing Group, Inc.

Cover design by Nelson Sá.

Library of Congress Cataloging-in-Publication Data

Gordon, Matthew.
Islam / Matthew S. Gordon.
     p. cm.—(Understanding religions)
Includes bibliographical references and index.
ISBN-13: 978-1-4358-5618-9 (library binding)
1. Islam—Juvenile literature. I. Title.
BP161.3.G669 2010
297—dc22

                                                        2009010043

Manufactured in Malaysia

Copyright © Duncan Baird Publishers
Text copyright © Duncan Baird Publishers
Commissioned artwork copyright © Duncan Baird Publishers

CONTENTS

INTRODUCTION

Islam is the last of the major monotheistic traditions to emerge in history. The term *Islam*, often translated as "submission," reflects the decision by the Muslim ("One who submits or surrenders") to abide in mind and body by the will of God (in Arabic, *Allah*, the "One God"). To submit to the divine will is therefore to bring about harmonious order to the universe. In this sense, Islam refers not simply to the act of submission but, more importantly, to its consequence—that is, peace (*salam*).

The Islamic tradition dates its origins to events that unfolded in the early seventh century CE in the Arabian town of Mecca. The tradition teaches that a forty-year-old merchant, Muhammad ibn Abdallah—commonly referred to as the Prophet, or Messenger, of God—received a series of revelations from God beginning in 610 CE and ending soon before his death in 632 CE. These revelations, collectively known as the Quran, are held by Muslims to be God's direct and inalterable word. The Quran is, in its own words, the symbol and embodiment of the intimate relationship between God and humankind: "This book, without doubt, is a guide to those in awe and fear [of God]" (*Sura* 2.2).

Complementing the Quran is the voluminous record of Muhammad's life known as the Hadith, which con-

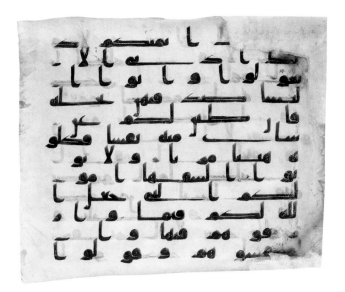

A folio from a massive Quran (21x26 inches/54x66 centimeters) produced in North Africa in the early 8th century CE. *This style of Arabic calligraphy is known as kufic.*

veys the *Sunna*, or "Tradition," of how the Prophet thought, spoke, and conducted his affairs. The Quran and the Hadith function in synthesis and together serve as the central source of Islamic religious and legal guidance. Those with the task of interpreting the Quran and the Hadith are known as the *ulama* ("learned ones"), or religious scholars. From their efforts emerged a complex code of regulations called the Sharia, which forms the basis of Islamic law.

The majority of contemporary Muslims are members of the Sunni community. This branch of Islam emerged by the tenth century CE from the scholarly circles of Damascus, Cairo, Baghdad, and the major Iranian cities. Sunni Islam took shape partly through the inevitable tendency among organized religious traditions to define what has been called "orthopraxy," and partly as a reaction to the articulation of other forms of Islam. Chief among these is Shiism, sometimes referred to as the "minority" community of Islam. Of the branches of Shia Islam, the largest is "Twelver" Shiism whose adherents form a majority in Iran and southern Iraq and a substantial minority in Lebanon, Kuwait, Pakistan, and elsewhere. The Ismaili Shias, who form particular sub-branches, are mainly located in India, East Africa, and, increasingly, urban Canada and the United Kingdom. The smaller branch of the Zaydis are represented principally in Yemen.

Islam, like other faiths, has been called a "cumulative tradition." It developed initially in the Near East but, thereafter, spread into such regions as Iran, India, Central Asia, and North Africa. At its earliest stage, it interacted with Hellenism, Judaism, and Christianity, with Zoroastrianism in Iran and the legal and political patterns of the Byzantine and Sassanian empires and the largely Turkic world of the Central Asian steppes. Today the Islamic community reflects a wide range of national, ethnic, socio-economic, and linguistic backgrounds.

A steadily growing proportion of the world's population adheres to the Islamic faith. The figure of one billion is often cited, although accurate figures are hard to come by in many regions where Muslims predominate. A common misconception is that most Muslims are Arabs, an idea derived from the fact that most Arabs are Muslims, the Near Eastern origins of the faith, and the close association of Arabic and the Quran. In fact, only some 18–21 percent of Muslims reside in the Arab world, while, of Muslims worldwide, some 80 percent or more are non-Arabs. The nation with the largest Muslim population is Indonesia, followed by Pakistan, Bangladesh, and India. Most Iranians and Turks are Muslims, as are significant populations in China, Russia, and sub-Saharan Africa. Europe and North America are home to steadily growing Muslim communities. Large numbers of Muslims of South Asian descent reside in the United Kingdom, many North African Muslims live in France and Belgium, and many Turks and Iranians have settled in Germany in recent decades. Islam in Europe and North America is also represented by increasing numbers of converts from non-immigrant communities.

CHAPTER ONE

ORIGINS AND HISTORICAL DEVELOPMENT

The Islamic tradition was born in the Arabian peninsula with the reception and dissemination of divine revelation by the Prophet Muhammad. Inspired by the Prophet's teachings, Arab forces extended the Islamic domain into the Near East and North Africa. Under the imperial rule of the Umayyad (661–750 CE) and Abbasid (750–1258 CE) dynasties, the tradition spread into Central Asia, India, and Spain.

By the tenth century, conversion to Islam had led to the emergence of a Muslim majority in North Africa, the Near East, and Central Asia, and by the eighteenth century Islam had embraced the modern-day states of Indonesia and Malaysia and was making strides in sub-Saharan Africa. In the modern period, Islam emerged as a dominant religion, the faith of millions of adherents worldwide.

LEFT: Interior of the 12th-century Kutubiyya mosque in Marrakech, Morocco. Built by the Almohad dynasty, it is one of North Africa's finest expressions of monumental architecture.

Muhammad ibn Abdallah belonged to the Arab cultural world that encompassed the Arabian peninsula and areas of southern Syria and Mesopotamia. Most inhabitants of Arabia were pastoral nomads who lived a demanding existence based on raiding and the rearing of lifestock. For nearly all Arabs, the tribe was the principal form of socio-political organization; it provided security and a sense of identity. Despite a common culture and a shared language (Arabic), no political unity existed among the tribes of Arabia.

The patterns of Arab life were shaped by political, economic, and religious currents of the wider Near East. Christian stories and practices were disseminated by merchants and others as they crisscrossed the peninsula. A Jewish presence is also attested, and Muhammad certainly had exposure to Judaic and Christian traditions. Rivalry over control of the Near East by the Byzantine and Sassanian empires was felt in Arabia as well. By the early seventh century, both empires were debilitated by war and internal dissent and were ill-prepared for campaigns launched from the Arabian hinterland.

The Islamic community, or *Umma*, to use the Quranic term, dates its foundation to Muhammad's prophetic mission, which began in 610 CE. At this time, the Quraysh tribe controlled the Haram (from the

Arabic for "inviolable"), the center of local religious practice and a place of pilgrimage that housed the ancient stone structure the Kaba (see p. 16, pp. 50–51, and p. 74). This was surrounded by idols representing such deities as Hubal, a war god, and the three daughters of Allah, the divine lord of the Haram. It was in the name of Allah that Muhammad initiated his teachings, although at this stage Allah was clearly accompanied by "associate" divinities. The use of the Haram by pilgrims thus overlapped with its use by merchants; it was seen to be neutral ground, where trade and religion could be conducted without interference.

The Meccan response to Muhammad's teachings turned hostile, no doubt due to his stress upon the pure monotheism of the Quran and his criticism of the Haram cult. In 622 CE, persecution of Muhammad's supporters led him to move them to the northern town of Yathrib. Muhammad and a close follower, Abu Bakr al-Siddiq, were the last to depart. The dramatic journey is known as the Hijra and is held by Islamic tradition to mark the establishment of the *Umma* as well as the beginning of the Islamic calendar (see pp. 81–87).

In Yathrib, known from then on as Medina, Muhammad continued his prophetic mission and consolidated his following. If attempts to win the backing of the Jews of Medina ended in tragedy (with the exile of two tribes and the destruction of the third), Muhammad's sympathetic leadership was very much on display following his triumph over the Meccans; in several gestures, he forgave the Qurayshi leadership for its resistance.

Shortly before his death (632 CE), Muhammad may have also initiated campaigns against the Byzantines in southern Syria. Under his successors, Muslim/Arab forces consolidated control over Arabia and then set out on campaigns that led to the destruction of the Sassanian monarchy and the ousting of Byzantine forces from Egypt and Syria. Subsequent conquests led to the spread of Islamic authority over Central Asia, northern India, North Africa, and the Iberian peninsula.

Conversion of subject peoples occurred steadily over several centuries, with majorities emerging in the Near East and North Africa. However, significant Jewish, Christian, and Zoroastrian communities remained. They came to be known as "Peoples of the Book," that is, peoples to whom God had revealed his prophetic message. They were termed *dhimmi*s, or the members of "protected" communities, by the Islamic establishment. This entailed a respect for their traditions and a guarantee of security of persons, property, and religious sites. On the other hand, their status was secondary to that of

Muslims. In many places, they were required to wear distinguishing clothing and were prohibited from propagating their faith. They were also usually obliged to pay a special poll tax (*jizya*). *Dhimmi* status may have compelled some non-Muslims to convert to Islam.

Rule over the empire was exerted initially by companions of the Prophet, then by the Umayyads, an elite Quraysh family. The successors to the Prophet bore the title "Caliph" (from the Arabic *khalifa*, "deputy" or "successor"). From 661 CE to 750 CE, and with the transfer of the imperial capital to Damascus, the Umayyads took significant steps toward the Arabization and Islamization of the conquered regions. The Umayyads were overthrown by the Abbasids, a branch of the Banu Hashim (the Prophet's clan). From Baghdad, built in the 760s, the Abbasids ruled throughout a period of steady growth in the Islamic community.

The expanding urban centers of the Islamic world witnessed a cross-fertilization of Arab, Jewish, Persian, and Hellenistic traditions. This mix, coupled with the demands of imperial administration, explains the remarkable flowering of Islamic legal, religious, political, and scientific thought. Baghdad was often the scene of the greatest activity. However, by the mid-ninth century, Abbasid authority began to slip. The dynasty

The Kaba, covered with a veil called the kiswa, *stands today at the center of a vast mosque, the size of which is testimony to the large numbers of pilgrims who participate in the Hajj.*

had already lost Spain more than a century earlier, and now political setbacks and the growing prominence of the *ulama* contributed to a loss of legitimation. No less serious was the challenge of the sectarian communities that represented the Shia branch of Islam. Most Muslims today adhere to Sunnism, which stresses consensus and community, based on the Quran and the prophetic model. The term "Sunni" derives from the Arabic for "people of the tradition [that is, the prophetic tradition, or *sunna*] and the community." The "tradition" is the example of Muhammad, the model for Muslim conduct. Key steps in the formalization of Sunnism include the emergence, by the eleventh century, of four major legal schools (see p. 62).

Shiism dates to the conflict that erupted upon the Prophet's death. Leading Muslims chose Abu Bakr as his successor—a decision that angered supporters of Ali ibn Abi Talib, the Prophet's son-in-law, whom they viewed as the only legitimate successor. He and his male descendants were later assigned roles closely tied to those of the Prophet, following the claim that only select male descendants of the Prophet's house could rightfully lead the community. Such individuals are known as Imams (see pp. 52–56).

The major divisions of Shia Islam, those of the "Twelvers" (see pp. 52–54) and of the Ismailis (see pp. 55–56), arose from disagreements over the identity of the Imams. Centered in Baghdad, the "Twelvers" were led by scholars who were well-integrated into urban society. Rural-based Ismaili Shiism took the form of a missionary movement. In North Africa, one Ismaili group established a state that came to be known as the Fatimid caliphate, a key rival of the Abbasid dynasty.

The Abbasid empire was gradually replaced by regional centers of authority. The Fatimids conquered Egypt in 969 CE and ruled from Cairo until the late twelfth century. In Central Asia and Iran, Abbasid rule gave way to nomadic Muslim Turkic forces, notably those of the Seljuqs, who, ruling as sultans, seized Baghdad in 1055 CE. A relatively brief period of Seljuq unity ended in fragmentation, but the stage was set for further Turkic invasions and ultimately the arrival of the Mongols in the thirteenth century. The most significant Turkish regime of the period was that of the Mamelukes of Egypt (1250–1517 CE).

Islamic rule first came to India with the early conquests, but an extensive presence arrived only in the thirteenth century with the "Delhi Sultanates" (1206–1526 CE). Muslim merchants, teachers, and Sufis spread the faith through India. Subsequent centuries witnessed Islam's spread into Southeast Asia, with majorities emerging in what are now Indonesia and Malaysia. Sufis and others carried Islam through the Sahara into Somalia and Tanzania. The main advances in sub-Saharan Africa occurred in the nineteenth and twentieth centuries.

The spread of Islam in the pre-modern period owes much, therefore, to official or state patronage. No less a source of Islamic teaching and example, as already indicated, were the efforts of Sufi orders to win followers.

Three dynamic and prosperous empires emerged in the Islamic world some time around the sixteenth century. Ruling from Istanbul (the former Byzantine capital of Constantinople), the Ottoman Turkish sultans came to control a domain that embraced coastal North Africa, the Near East and Egypt, and much of southeastern Europe. The Safavid dynasty in Iran brought about the gradual conversion of much of Iranian society to "Twelver" Shia Islam. The Mughal dynasty in India ran an officially Islamic state, but relied upon the support of Hindu society.

The eighteenth century brought wrenching change to the Islamic world. The Ottomans, Safavids, and Mughals were beset with internal troubles and challenges from the European imperial powers of Britain, France, and Russia. European imperialism led to the occupation, by the early twentieth century, of many Islamic regions. Concerns over the fragmentation of the Islamic world—understood in spiritual as well as economic and political terms—informs the work of Muslim scholars and activists down to the present day.

Ibn Battuta's *Travels in Asia and Africa 1325–1354*

" During my stay at Alexandria I had heard of the pious Shaykh al-Murshidi, who bestowed gifts miraculously created at his desire. He lived in solitary retreat in a cell in the country where he was visited by princes and ministers . . . .That night while I was sleeping on the roof of the cell, I dreamed that I was on the wing of a great bird which was flying with me towards Mecca, then to Yemen, then eastwards, and thereafter going towards the south, then flying far eastwards, and finally landing in a dark and green country, where it left me. I was astonished at this dream and said to myself 'If the shaykh can interpret my dream for me, he is all they say he is.' Next morning, after all the other visitors had gone, he called me and when I had related my dream interpreted it to me saying: 'You will make the pilgrimage [to Mecca] and visit [the tomb of] the Prophet, and you will travel through Yemen, Iraq, the country of the Turks, and India.' "

From *Ibn Battuta: Travels in Asia and Africa 1325–1354*. Translated and selected by H.A.R. Gibb. Routledge & Kegan Paul Ltd: London, 1957, pp. 47–48.

Commentary

One invaluable source of information on the medieval Islamic world, specifically that of the fourteenth century, is the travel account of the scholar Ibn Battuta (died ca. 1370 CE). Born in Tangiers in 1304 CE, he set out on a pilgrimage to Mecca as a young man. Crossing North Africa to the Hijaz, he then journeyed on to Palestine, Syria, Iran, into Central Asia and ultimately to East Africa, India, Southeast Asia and, possibly, China.

His detailed account speaks to the vast array of cultures, languages, traditions, and histories that informed Islamic societies in that period. He records the effects upon Persia and Central Asia of the thirteenth-century Mongol invasions; the spread of Islam among the Turkic peoples (then gradually occupying the Anatolian peninsula); and the growing presence of the tradition in the lands bordering the Indian Ocean and within Africa.

The passage underscores the centrality of Mecca to Islamic practice and imagination. Referred to often in Islamic letters as *al-mukarrima* ("the blessed"), Mecca is the birthplace of the Prophet Muhammad, site of the revelation of the Quran, and location of the sacred Kaba. No less critically, Mecca is also where, during every pilgrimage season (see pp. 85–86), Muslims gather to celebrate their faith as a community.

CHAPTER TWO

ASPECTS OF THE DIVINE

A central feature of any religion is what may be termed the "divine," or, in other words, a reality that is greater than human. How this reality is defined in Islam, and the manner in which God is conceived of and approached by his devotees, gives us a clearer insight into the tradition.

According to Islam, as an expression of his infinite mercy and concern for humankind, God revealed his will and his guidance on how to live in the world in the Quran—it is in this sacred text that his awesome presence is made explicit: "God is He who has raised the skies without support, as you can see, and established Himself upon His throne, and subjected the sun and the moon to His will . . . . He regulates all matters." (*Sura* 13.2).

LEFT: *A devotee beside the* mihrab *(prayer niche) of a mosque associated with one of the various Sufi orders.*

Islam conceives of God as that from which all else emanates. The term for God in the Quran is Allah, which means, simply, "the [one] god" (*al-ilah*): "God bears witness that there is no god but He, as do the angels and those possessing knowledge. He acts but with justice. There is no god but He, the all-Mighty, the all-Wise" (*Sura* 3.18).

The relationship between Muslims and God is informed by three principles that derive directly from the Quran. The first principle, *tawhid*, might be rendered simply as "the unity of God." According to this central Islamic idea, he is utterly and inevitably One, a perfect unity, unique unto himself. However, a more accurate translation would be "the affirmation of the divine unity," which encompasses the crucial responsibility of Muslims to inform their faith (*iman*) and its practice (*islam*) with their belief in the awesome justice and unity of the divine. Thus *tawhid* ("divine unity") becomes a summons to an attentive and pious life.

Knowledge of God and his will is deemed essential to Muslim life. A key Quranic theme is that God reveals himself through "signs" (*ayat*). The Quran itself is such a sign, as is every verse, phrase, and word of the sacred book. Each sign bears information about God and his creative power—to learn about God, therefore, every effort must be made to recognize and grasp these signs. In practical terms, this means that reading and studying the Quran are essential activities.

God is served by a host of angels and by mysterious beings known as *jinn* (a collective noun, the origin of the term "genie"). Faith in God includes belief in the work performed by the angels on his behalf. Several of the angels are named in the Quran and, of this group, Gabriel stands as the most prominent. For example, it is Gabriel who is said to have brought the Quran to Muhammad. The angels, described as the creatures made of light, were joined at a critical juncture by one of the *jinn*, the creatures of fire, known as Iblis (Satan). At this moment, Adam was created. In response to God's command to prostrate themselves before the newly fashioned being, all but Iblis obey—as a result of this act of defiance, he is cast from heaven and made to devote his time to drawing humans away from God.

Nubuwwa, or "prophecy," is the second principle upon which the Muslim's relationship to God is based. It refers to the manner in which God offers guidance to the world and makes clear his will. In treating faith, Muslim scholars stress that it must include belief in the prophets and the prophetic message that communicates the divine will to humankind. The doctrine encompasses all of the books of divine revelation, including the Torah of Moses and the Gospel of Jesus, both of which are lauded in the Quran for precisely this reason. Each is a summons to proper obeisance and worship. However, of all the prophets, Islam accords Muhammad a special role as the "seal" of prophecy (see pp. 49–50).

The ideas of "divine unity" and "prophecy" are expressed in a statement known as the Shahada: "There is no god but God [Allah], and Muhammad is His messenger." Uttering the Shahada is all that is required in order to convert to Islam, and it is traditionally whispered into the ears of a newborn child. It is also the first of the set of ritual duties known as the "Five Pillars," the acts upon which the ritual system of Islam rests (see pp. 63–65).

The third principle concerns the concept of the "Last Days," or the end of the world, and is often expressed by the term *maad*, or "return," which conveys the idea that all God's creations will ultimately return to their divine source. The Quran makes clear, often in vivid terms, that the Last Days will be accompanied by the Final Judgment and states that everyone will be assessed on the character of their response to the prophetic summons. Faith, as it is conceived in Islamic teaching, includes belief in divine judgment and in the eternal reward or suffering that ensues.

The Shia tradition articulates two further principles, those of the "imamate" and of *adl*, or "divine justice." The first principle holds that a specific group of divinely inspired descendants from the Prophet's house carried on Muhammad's social and spiritual leadership. These individuals are known as the Imams (see pp. 52–56) and are viewed as the only legitimate leaders of the Islamic community. *Adl*, the second principle, represents perfect justice as a key attribute of God and brings together two ideas: divine judgment as the expression of that perfect justice, and humans as being fully responsible for their actions.

In Islamic teaching, the violation of *tawhid* is known as *shirk*, often translated as "association"—that is, associating any aspect of the world with the divine when it does not, and cannot, possess these qualities. The Quran is clear on this point: "Serve God and do not associate anything with Him" (*Sura* 4.36). The failure to worship God alone may take the form of veneration of another presence or being in the universe. Muslim scholars have also interpreted *shirk* as a preoccupation with material wealth, and as impulsive and arrogant behavior toward others—in such cases, the individual's attitude to God, and his or her standing within the Islamic community, would be corrupted.

An 18th-century steel standard head from southern Iran bearing, in the center, the first part of the Shahada: "There is no god but God."

From the earliest days of Islamic history, Muslim scholars have wrestled with the many issues surrounding knowledge, or awareness, of God. For example, a debate erupted in the ninth century CE concerning the extent to which God was discernible through the use of reason, and was the result of a long period of translation and commentary by Muslims of Greek works of philosophy and science.

Islamic art was also shaped by concerns over human knowledge of God. The claim that the Islamic tradition has always forbidden representational art is misleading, if not simply false. The Islamic world boasts a rich tradition of illustrated manuscripts (excluding the Quran and other purely religious works). Although the Quran contains no explicit ban on such work, a predominantly hostile attitude developed

among Muslim scholars toward any sort of representational imagery. This attitude was based on the argument
that the representation of living beings challenges the
creative genius that God alone possesses. Thus no
representational art appears in mosques, where, instead,
the magnificent Islamic traditions of calligraphy and
symbolic art flourish.

However, a far more significant dimension of the
Islamic tradition has been the quest for a heightened
spiritual awareness of the divine. Sufism, often translated as Islamic mysticism, is the term usually assigned
to the search for inner spirituality and proximity to God.
The word may derive from the Arabic *suf* ("wool"), and
is perhaps a reference to the rough, simple garb worn
by ascetics in the formative period of Islam.

In the Muslim context, this search for inner or
spiritual awareness should be viewed as an integral
dimension of Islamic life rather than as something pursued apart from the mainstream practices and doctrines
of the tradition. Sufism drew much of its initial inspiration from the Quranic idea of "friendship" (*wilaya*)
with God, and Sufis are therefore often referred to in
Islamic letters as the "friends" (*waliya*, singular *wali*) of
God. They are, in other words, those who are sincere and
utterly trusting in their relationship with the divine.

The origins of Sufism extend back to the practices of the Prophet and his companions. Islamic literature draws a vivid portrait of Muhammad's simple, ascetic lifestyle and the manner in which his example inspired even the elite of the early Islamic empire, including the caliphs. In Sufi texts, Muhammad emerges as the exemplar of the inner, spiritual life, and later Sufi poets and writers cited as their most convincing evidence for this the miraculous journey (the Isra) of the Prophet from Mecca to Jerusalem and thence to heaven (the Miraj; see p. 50).

Drawing on the prophetic example and the teachings of revelation, the early Sufis began to articulate ideas that later thinkers would develop into theoretical Sufism, a key branch of medieval Islamic letters. These ideas are associated with such early figures as Hasan al-Basri (died 728 CE), Rabia al-Adawiya (died 801 CE), al-Tustari (died 896 CE), and Junayd (died 910 CE). The first two figures stressed the value of asceticism, an unwavering trust in the divine purpose, and self-awareness. Later Sufi thinkers, such as al-Hujwiri (died 1075 CE) and al-Ghazali (died 1111 CE), contributed more systematic, formal works to Islamic spiritual literature and stressed discipline and contemplation as being essential to the spiritual life. More controversial was the conviction that true dedication to such a "quest" could lead to the union of the self with the divine presence, sometimes described as the annihilation of the self (*fana*).

Through the ideas and reputation of these early ascetics, Sufism attracted a growing number of followers. In the ninth and tenth centuries CE, there emerged informal circles of teachers, or "guides" (*shaykh*s), and their students (*murid*s). Their experience generated the key idea that the inner life was shaped by a disciplined progress through a series of spiritual stages, to each of which the student was led by his or her teacher or master. Just as the master derived knowledge and guidance through trust in God, so too would the student from his or her *shaykh*.

Central to the spiritual search of Sufism is the practice of *dhikr*, often translated as "remembering" or "invoking" God and his names, either in silent meditation or quiet chanting. The origin of *dhikr* lies in the Quran and in the Hadith of the Prophet (see pp. 42–43), and is epitomized in the ritual prayer, or *salat*, in which Muslims invoke the presence and names of God. The Quran provides a long series of names for God, each of which expresses a new dimension of the ultimately indescribable divine presence. In a famous Hadith, the Prophet refers to ninety-nine names of God, although the Quran can be read as listing many others. These are not simply a list of characteristics but constitute one way in which the Quran communicates the idea of God's perfection; each quality may be partially possessed by humans but only God can possess them all, perfectly and completely. Two names perhaps stand out: *al-Rahman* ("the All-Compassionate") and *al-Rahim* ("the All-Merciful").

Early Sufism was largely confined to small, ascetic circles, which often operated in urban centers. But by the tenth and eleventh centuries, its ideas had begun to spread into the broader community. Sufi orders began to take shape, as did lodges (*khanqah*s), which were used by their members in ever greater numbers. Within several centuries, Sufi orders became an everyday feature of Islamic life, and remain so today in many regions.

Many historians consider the Qadiriyya to be among the very first of the major Sufi orders to emerge. The name derives from Abd al-Qadir al-Jilani (died 1166 CE), a Persian scholar and preacher, whose sermons in Baghdad are said to have attracted a large following. His sons and other early disciples laid the groundwork for the order, as well as for the growth in his reputation—many pilgrims still visit his tomb today.

Other early orders include the Suhrawardiyya and Shadhiliyya groups, the first of which is important in modern-day India, Pakistan, and Bangladesh, the second traditionally prominent in North Africa and the Near East. The Bektashiyya, a Turkish order closely associated with the military of the former Ottoman empire, was known for its esoteric practices, as was the Rifaiyya, a branch of the Qadiriyya, whose members sometimes ate glass and walked on hot coals. These prominent organizations played a critical part in winning converts to Islam in many regions of central Africa, the Indian Ocean, and Central Asia.

God and the many divine characteristics are the subject of an extensive body of writings by medieval and modern theologians, mystics, poets, and novelists. Among the great medieval Islamic thinkers is Abu Hamid Muhammad al-Ghazali (1058–1111 CE), whose works remain widely read today. Of Persian origin, he pursued a lifetime of teaching and writing, interrupted by a decade of contemplation and travel occasioned by a spiritual crisis. His best-known work, and a significant expression of Sunni Muslim faith, is the voluminous *Ihya Ulum al-Din* ("The Revival of the Religious Sciences"). In this and other works, including his famous spiritual biography, *al-Munqidh min al-Dalal* ("Deliverance from Error"), al-Ghazali achieved a kind of synthesis of rational and spiritual approaches to the worship of God.

Surat al-Fatiha

" In the name of God, the Merciful, the Compassionate.

Praise be to God, the Lord of all being.

The Merciful, the Compassionate.

Master of the Day of Judgment.

It is You alone that we serve,

It is only from You that we seek aid.

Guide us on the straight path.

The path of those whom You have blessed.

Not of those with whom You are displeased,

Nor of those who go astray. **"**

From the Quran, translated by Matthew S. Gordon.

Commentary

A succinct statement, the opening *sura* of the Quran communicates essential ideas of the Islamic tradition. God, as "Lord of all being (or 'of the worlds')," stands above and utterly distinct from the world. In this sense, the attributes assigned to him can only approximate his qualities of mercy, compassion, and creative power. However, for all that he is apart, He is forever present and aware, and thus the only appropriate responses are praise and worship. The *sura* also makes clear that humans must shoulder responsibility for the choices presented to them. They may choose to worship God or, as the *sura* puts it, to remain on "the path," and thus receive divine guidance, or they may venture away, be it out of carelessness or deliberate refusal to heed that guidance. Any number of verses in the Quran associate God with the direction that he provides and many draw upon the image of the Straight Path. The image thus appears throughout Islamic literature, exegetical and otherwise. As the Quran itself puts it, the Path is the way from darkness into the light. Elsewhere it is depicted as the path upon which all human beings will go on the day of resurrection. In this case, it is described as a razor-sharp bridge stretched over the flames of hell that only the righteous can expect to cross without tumbling into the depths.

The *Surat al-Fatiha* is often compared, in terms of both content and daily use, to the Lord's Prayer in the Christian tradition. A short text, it is easily memorized at a young age and is then commonly and frequently recited by Muslims at all stages of life. In this sense, it is one of several verbal formulas or phrases—short or long—that punctuate the speech of Muslims. A common phrase is *al-salamu allaykum* or "peace be upon you," which is used typically only among Muslims.

CHAPTER THREE

SACRED TEXTS

The Islamic tradition considers the Quran to be the literal word of God, directly transmitted to the Prophet over the course of his adult life. Muslims acknowledge the Quran as the extension of the divine into the earthly realm, the embodiment on Earth of God's mercy, power, and mystery.

To guide them in interpreting the Quran, the religious scholars, or *ulama*, relied on the vast collection of reports that contain the Prophet's teachings, words, and deeds. This collection, known as the Hadith, acts as an additional source of divine wisdom and guidance alongside the Quran. A separate body of Hadith—known as Hadith Qudsi—contains sayings that have come directly from God. The Quran and the Hadith are the two principal sources used to articulate Islamic law and doctrine.

LEFT: Boys at the Fouad Islamic Institute, a Quranic school in Assyut, Egypt. Instruction in the Quran continues to form an important part of the education of most Muslims.

The word *quran* means "recitation," and can refer to a part or the whole of the sacred text. The verses of the Quran were revealed to Muhammad who, over the course of his prophetic mission, recited and explained them to his followers. According to the Islamic tradition, the Quran achieved its present, written form during the caliphate of Uthman (644–656 CE), who ordered a group of respected Muslims to create a definitive version. It is composed of one hundred and fourteen chapters known as *sura*s, each of which bears both a number and a title, the latter usually a word or phrase occurring early in the *sura*; for example, *Sura 2, al-Baqara* ("The Cow"). While Western scholars tend to cite Quranic chapters by number, Muslim writers generally refer to their titles.

The *sura*s are composed of individual verses (*ayat*, singular *aya*), each of which is seen to be a "sign" from God of his presence and mercy (see pp. 24–25). The tradition holds that the first *sura* to be revealed to Muhammad was *Sura 96, al-Alaq* ("The Blood-Clot"), spoken to the Prophet by the angel Gabriel. It represents the announcement to Muhammad of his mission: "Recite: in the name of your Lord who created, who created Man from a blood-clot" (96.1–2; that is, *Sura 96, ayat* 1–2). The *sura*s are ordered according to length, with the longest at the beginning of the Quran, and the shorter ones toward the end.

Sura *1,* al-Fatiha *("The Opening") (right) and the first page of* Sura *2,* al-Baqara *("The Cow"), from a decorated Quran produced in Mughal India, ca. 1700.*

One exception is *Sura* 1, *al-Fatiha* ("The Opening"), which has seven verses and opens the Quran. Every *sura*, except for one, begins with the invocation known as the *Basmala* or *Bismillah*: "In the name of God, the Merciful, the Compassionate." This phrase is also uttered at the start of every act of worship.

The *sura*s are also identified as either "Meccan" or "Medinan," depending on whether they were revealed before or after the Hijra, Muhammad's departure for Medina in 622 CE. The Meccan verses tend to center on God's majesty and unity and the certainty that he is to bring his compassion and judgment to bear upon humanity and the world.

Muhammad's role in the Meccan period, as he himself proclaimed, was to deliver glad tidings of God's compassion, and to warn of the coming judgment that would separate the righteous from the wrongdoers: "For those who disbelieve will come a fearsome punishment, for those who believe and do good will come forgiveness and reward" (*Sura* 35.7). The Meccan verses are often short and succinct, with vivid, intense imagery.

The Medinan verses contain similar ideas and language, but reflect the challenges confronting the newly established Islamic community under Muhammad's leadership. They are generally longer and more complex and often express a concern for the religious, moral, and social order. More importantly, they prescribe the central duties of Islam: prayer, alms, fasting at Ramadan, and the pilgrimage to Mecca (the Hajj). They also address such issues as marriage, divorce, adultery, gambling, and the waging of war.

The Quran is present in the everyday life of Muslims in a variety of ways. Traditionally, it has been the focus of Islamic education, with young Muslims learning to read and write Quranic verses and memorizing and reciting the entire text. Although this practice has fallen victim over the last century to the spread of largely secular public schooling, parents today still try to ensure that their children receive Quranic learning. The Prophet's own example of oral transmission of the word of God helps to explain the great value attached to memorization and recitation. Quranic recitation remains a cherished art form, and recordings by noted reciters are readily available throughout the Islamic world. Muslims attach a physical sacredness to the Quran and prefer to handle it only in a state of ritual purity; they also believe it to possess a divine power or grace (*baraka*) that can, in more popular usage, be employed in healing rituals.

It is therefore not surprising to discover that, from early in Islamic history, the *ulama* have devoted tremendous efforts to elucidating the complex teachings of the Quran. Quranic interpretation, or *tafsir*, forms part of the core of Islamic learning. Works of *tafsir* abound in Islamic letters; one of the earliest, and mostly highly regarded, is the multivolume opus of Muhammad ibn Jarir al-Tabari (839–923 CE), a Baghdadi scholar of

Persian origin. The work contains a close reading of the language of the Quran as well as detailed consideration of the legal and theological meanings of the text. In this sense, it is both a profound statement of faith and a signal contribution to Islamic scholarship.

To guide them in interpreting the Quran, the religious scholars relied on the vast corpus of traditions concerning Muhammad himself. On his death, the Islamic community set about collecting and preserving reports that contain both his teachings and descriptions of his deeds. The Prophet's "way" or "tradition" is known as the *Sunna* or "exemplary practice." The reports themselves, which were assembled and organized in the first few centuries of Islamic history, are known, collectively and individually, as Hadith. An essential role was played in their compilation by the family members and close companions of the Prophet from whom the community initially acquired this information. In its final form, each Hadith was headed by a list of those through whom the report was transmitted, which ideally extended back to Muhammad or to a close companion to whom he had spoken directly.

The key period of Hadith collection and commentary was the late eighth to early ninth century CE. Muslim scholars also closely analyzed the myriad reports then circulating within the growing Islamic community. The Hadith generated much debate in early medieval times since it became clear to scholars that many of the Hadith reflected opinions or doctrinal positions that postdated the Prophet's lifetime. In the Sunni world, the most respected Hadith collections are those of al-Bukhari (810–870 CE) and Muslim ibn al-Hajjaj (died 875 CE).

Shiism also generated a large and complex body of Hadith going back through the Imams (see pp. 52–56) as well as through the Prophet. For Shia scholars, the Hadith of the Imams play an identical role to that of the Sunni Hadith—namely, to elucidate the Quran and to serve as a source of religious and legal thought. Of four early and important collections of Hadith, perhaps the most significant is that of al-Kulayni (died 939 CE).

The reports of the prophetic *Sunna* are essential to Islamic practice. Muslims must devote themselves, in every realm of life, to "right" or proper conduct—it is only in this way that Muslims, and Muslim society, can function in a manner that is commensurate with the divine will. The *Sunna* not only provides the teachings of the Prophet to Muslims in such areas as, for example, ritual (with the Prophet serving as instructor), but also, in a more general sense, offers a model for the properly pious and humble existence.

Surat al-Maidah ("The Table," 5.48)

66 To you We have sent down the Book,

In truth, confirming the scripture that came before it,

And watching over it with care.

So judge between them on the basis of what God

Has sent down,

And do not follow their false desires

And so venture astray from what has come to you of

the Truth.

To each among you We have revealed a Law

And a Clear Path. 99

From the Quran, translated by Matthew S. Gordon.

Commentary

The Quran stands apart from Jewish and Christian scripture in one interesting respect: as this extract reveals, the
Quran often comments on itself—that is, on its own significance and meaning. It refers to itself as the direct and
unaltered revelation from God communicated to
Muhammad (through Gabriel) in Arabic. It is, by its very
nature, the greatest miracle in Islam and to Muslims it
represents the extension of the divine presence into the
physical world. Thus, as scholars have so often pointed
out, the Quran is to Islam what Christ is to Christianity.

The Quran stresses its relationship with the scriptures of Judaism and Christianity; it represents, as do those texts, divine guidance and authority. It teaches that, since the dawn of time, God has communicated to humankind through a series of prophets, among whom stand Noah, Abraham, David, Moses, Jesus, and Muhammad. Each of the "books" sent to these figures contains the same essential message—that of divine unity and of the duty to worship. In this sense, the Quran was sent down to confirm the earlier revelations. It is another great manifestation of the message sent originally to Abraham.

However, the Quran makes it clear that in other respects it stands apart. One distinction made by Muslim interpreters of the Quran is to emphasize that, while each of the earlier texts communicates the "primordial" doctrine of divine unity, each also contains a unique emphasis—for example, the message to Moses stresses the law as the basis of human life, whereas that associated with Jesus emphasizes spirituality and love of God. The genius of Islam, according to this line of argument, lies in its expression of the primordial message through an integration of both the divine law and the inner, or spiritual, commitment to the divine. Thus, the Quran represents the completion, indeed the perfection, of divine revelation.

CHAPTER FOUR

SACRED PERSONS

Muslims often learn about their faith through stories, legends, poems, and songs that relate to persons whose lives reflect the workings of God and exhibit such qualities as piety, humility, determination, and wisdom. Of these words and deeds that reflect divine purpose, the most significant are those of the prophets. The Islamic tradition venerates such figures as Noah, Abraham, Moses, and Jesus—but it is undoubtedly Muhammad who stands at center stage.

The Shia tradition includes among its human exemplars select lines of male descendants from the Prophet's house—the Imams. More controversial, certainly in the modern Muslim world, is the role played throughout the Islamic tradition by local holy figures to whom the word "saint" is often applied.

LEFT: A depiction of the winged beast Buraq, with an empty saddle, on which Muhammad ascended to heaven. Buraq's guide, the angel Gabriel, hovers in front. From a 16th-century Ottoman Turkish manuscript of the Aja'ib al-Makhluqat *of Qazvini.*

The Prophet is revered as the model of the human life. His career is set out in a series of early Islamic texts that include the Hadith literature, biographies, and historical works such as the great *History of Prophets and Kings* by the ninth-century historian al-Tabari. The Quran stands, of course, as a unique account of the Prophet's existence: it is both a record of the event of divine revelation and a valuable—if often difficult to interpret—source of references to his life and prophetic mission (see pp. 12–14 and 49–51). The biographies of Muhammad constitute a genre known as Sira—the most significant example is by the eighth-century scholar Muhammad ibn Ishaq (died ca. 770 CE), which survives only in a later edition by Abd al-Malik ibn Hisham (died ca. 834 CE). The early biographies and the Hadith served as the basis of later elaborate accounts, in a variety of genres, of the Prophet's achievements. "Popular" accounts include songs and poetry that are performed to mark his birthday (Mawlid al-nabi; see p. 83) and other occasions.

According to biographers, Muhammad was born in Mecca in 570 CE into the Banu Hashim clan of the Quraysh tribe and orphaned at an early age. Reared by his extended family, he acquired, early on, a reputation for probity that earned him the nickname *al-Amin* ("the Trustworthy"). It is also said that a series of predictions revealed the remarkable course that his life was to take. His reputation caught the attention of an older woman, Khadija, a merchant who became his first wife. Their daughters included Fatima, revered by Shia Muslims— she and her husband (the Prophet's cousin), Ali ibn Abi Talib, and their sons, Hasan and Husayn, are significant as the source of the line of the Imams.

The members of Muhammad's household are known by the term *ahl al-bayt* (literally, "family of the house"). Several women who were to play a critical role in the Prophet's life are held up as especially deserving of praise. Khadija, his first wife, is remembered for having encouraged the Prophet during the initial moments of revelation when he was nearly overcome by the vision of the angel Gabriel. A later wife, Aisha, was more controversial. Sunnis recognize her as Muhammad's favorite wife after Khadija, but the Shia tradition claims she committed adultery and took part in civil unrest following the Prophet's death.

Muhammad's prophetic mission began in a cave on Mount Hira overlooking Mecca. In 610 CE, the angel Gabriel is said to have appeared to him with a summons to prophethood. Overcoming his initial terror, Muhammad began to teach the monotheisitic message that had been revealed to him, attracting a small following at first, but then drawing a larger public. Initially, Muhammad enjoyed the protection of his uncle and the support of Khadija in the face of growing opposition from the Meccans. The death of Khadija and Abu Talib in 619 CE left him increasingly vulnerable to attack, so, in 622 CE he carried out the journey to Medina (the former Yathrib) known as the Hijra.

The Hijra occurred shortly after an event that, for many Muslims, is proof of the Prophet's remarkable standing. According to early biographers, he was summoned by the angel Gabriel to go on a miraculous journey from the Kaba in Mecca to Jerusalem astride a wondrous, winged beast named Buraq. This event is known as the Isra. In the Holy City, Muhammad led the prophets, from Adam to Jesus, in prayer. He then ascended—an event known as the Miraj—through the seven heavens, visited hell and paradise, and, alone, entered into the divine presence.

In Medina, he quickly assumed new and often daunting responsibilities; he had been a prophet and teacher in Mecca, but now he was also the head of a growing community that required physical protection and guidance in social and legal affairs. Under his leadership, the Muslims defeated the Meccans and in 630 CE Mecca surrendered. On reentering the city of his birth,

Muhammad made his way to the Kaba (see pp. 12–13), which he purged of pre-Islamic idols, and thus purified. He also forged alliances with powerful tribes throughout Arabia, which was a crucial step in organizing the Arab tribes for the initial stages of the Islamic conquests.

Following his last pilgrimage to Mecca, shortly before his death, the Prophet is said to have delivered a final address to his followers at a place called Ghadir Khumm. The content of this address remains a source of division within the Islamic world to the present day. There is agreement that he commended his son-in-law, Ali ibn Abi Talib, to the community. But the Shia tradition holds that he also designated Ali as his successor. Shias believe, therefore, that Ali had the only legitimate claim to succeed the Prophet as leader (*imam*) of the young community and that the Muslim leadership directly violated the Prophet's wishes by choosing another man—Abu Bakr al-Siddiq—to succeed him. The term Shia, or Shiite, derives from the phrase *Shiat Ali* ("partisans" or "followers" of Ali).

Divisions between the Shias and the majority community only increased with the establishment of the Umayyad dynasty. After Ali's death, his followers turned their loyalties to his son, Hasan, then to Hasan's brother, Husayn. In 680 CE, in a bid to challenge Umayyad authority, Husayn attempted to join his family's partisans in the southern Iraqi town of Kufa. The Umayyad caliph Yazid ibn Muawiya (died 683 CE) dispatched troops to suppress the movement. Husayn and his male supporters were slaughtered at Karbala, near Kufa.

Building on this early, tragic history, Shia scholars developed a complex set of doctrines centered on the office of the imamate. The person of the Imam, as described in Shia literature, is a link in the chain of prophecy extending to Muhammad from Abraham and Jesus. He must be a direct descendant of Muhammad (through his daughter Fatima and Ali) and a designated successor of the Imam before him. The Imam is the only legitimate authority on Earth, and obedience to him is required of humankind. He is held to be infallible, without sin, and in possession of a body of knowledge transmitted by God through the Imams.

By far the largest Shia branch is "Twelver" Shiism, so called because of the belief in the person of the Twelfth Imam, a boy named Muhammad who is said to have gone into hiding after the death, in 873 CE, of his father, the Eleventh Imam, Hasan al-Askari. The Twelfth Imam's disappearance was explained not by his death but rather by his entry into a miraculous state of concealment, the nature and duration of which is known only to God. He therefore remains a living being to whom obedience is due from adherents of the tradition. The "hidden" Twelfth Imam is also viewed as a messianic figure who will return shortly before the Day of Judgment to lead the forces of good against those of evil in a final apocalyptic battle. He is frequently referred to as the "Imam Mahdi," *mahdi* being the most common Islamic term for messiah. Islamic ideas concerning the apocalyptic events surrounding the return of the Mahdi also often refer to the return of Christ, which is a further indication of the close association between Christian and Islamic doctrines.

Initially, the "Twelver *ulama*" (religious scholars), in the absence of the Imam himself, were content to play a limited role as teachers and spiritual guides to their community. However, as time went on it became increasingly clear that the scholars would also have to carry out, if only temporarily (that is, until the return of the "Awaited Imam"), the Imam's functions as leader of the community and source of legal and doctrinal rulings. Over the course of centuries, the "Twelver" *ulama* elaborated a clear definition of their role as representatives of the "hidden" Imam. As a consequence of this, the Imam's full legal and religious authority came to be bestowed upon the leading scholars of the day to whom the community was obliged to pay alms. The combination of economic power and religious authority endowed these men with considerable influence not only in relation to their constituent communities but also to local political elites where "Twelver" Shiism predominated.

An Iranian banner, ca. 1900, depicting the martyrdoms of al-Husayn (top left) and al-Hasan (mounted) at Karbala.

A second branch of the Shia tradition—the Ismaili branch—emerged following the death of Jafar al-Sadiq, the Sixth Imam, in 765 CE. While many of his followers supported his son, Musa, to succeed him as the Seventh Imam, others backed his eldest son, Ismail—hence this branch is known as the Ismailis, or "Seveners." The Ismailis generally believe in an unbroken line of Imams to the present day, unlike the "Twelvers" who await the

return of the "hidden" Imam. Ismaili Shiism has itself generated a number of subsects. One offshoot is the Druze religion. Originally an Ismaili group, the Druze ascribed divine standing to a member of the Fatimid dynasty. Attempts to eradicate what was perceived to be a heresy failed and today the tradition represents a sizeable minority in Lebanon, Syria, and northern Palestine.

Throughout the Islamic world, the belief persists that individuals and family lineages can be privileged with special spiritual powers or with a proximity to the holy. There is considerable overlap between the veneration of such "saints" and the more popular aspects of Sufism (see pp. 29–33), including the use of the Quranic term *wali Allah* ("friend of God") for both Sufis and Muslim "saints" alike.

The Islamic scholarly world has often displayed an uneasiness, even a marked hostility, toward such beliefs and the practices associated with them. Their reactions are generally based on the view that holiness should be ascribed to God alone, never to human beings. For many ordinary Muslims, however, the idea of "saints," or holiness in humans, is unobjectionable and the veneration of such figures has formed a significant part of their religious and spiritual lives to the present day. These beliefs can center on the "saint's" piety and moral standing or upon his or her ability to transform the physical world (for example, through healing) or to summon the natural elements. Present in many areas of the Islamic world is the belief in *baraka*—a spiritual blessing that can be transmitted to the follower from a "saint" or a "saint's" relics (such as his or her tomb). Other holy figures appear more as folk heroes, renowned, for example, for their resistance to oppressive rulers.

Islamic history has witnessed the emergence of many different cults around such figures, both at the local and international level. For example, the southern Moroccan city of Marrakech—which is often referred to as "the tomb of the saints," owing to the large number of holy persons who are buried there—is associated in particular with seven "saints" whose birthdays are celebrated in small neighborhood festivals. In contrast, the Egyptian figure Sayyid Ahmad al-Badawi (died 1276 CE) is renowned throughout Egypt and in neighboring countries. Several annual festivals are held in his honor, the most significant of which, at Tanta in Egypt, brings together large numbers of celebrants. In Karachi, Pakistan, many devotees flock to the tomb of Abd Shah Ghazi, another "saint"-like figure. Occasions such as these play an important role in the religious lives of local Muslim communities.

Praise Poem (*na't*) for Muhammad

" You are the ruler of this world and the next,

O Muhammad the chosen.

You are the leader of the Muslims, O Muhammad

the chosen.

You are the governor of the stable religion,

O Muhammad the chosen.

You are the *qibla* of those with firm conviction,

O Muhammad the chosen.

On the night of the *mi'raj*, you illuminated

the heavens;

On account of your footsteps the highest heaven and

divine throne

Became luminous and radiant.

The color and fragrance of the paradisiacal rose gardens

increased markedly;

In a place yonder that is beyond the imagination of

the angels

You are the reigning prince, O Muhammad the chosen. **"**

From *Windows on the House of Islam*, edited by John Renard. University of California Press: Berkeley, 1998, p. 124.

Commentary

These lines are extracted from an Urdu poem by the Indian writer Nazir Akbarabadi (died 1831). As they suggest, Muhammad has long been the subject of various but closely related forms of devotion in Islamic life. He is cherished as a reminder of divine guidance and as a source of guidance himself. References to Muhammad, whether scholarly or "popular," speak of him as the culmination of prophecy, its perfect embodiment. His relationship to God and the Quran lead Muslims to speak of him also as the perfect teacher and companion. Finally, he is venerated as the ideal Muslim, the perfect *abd* ("servant") of God. He offers, in other words, the means by which to model conduct and thought—understood, of course, in both an ethical and spiritual sense.

The verse cited here also refers to the Miraj, Muhammad's miraculous ascent, an event commemorated in ritual observances usually on the 27th of Rajab (the seventh Islamic month). Most of the later literature concerning the Prophet's journey relies directly on key Quranic passages that refer to the preceding journey (the Isra) as well as the early biographies and Hadith. The seventeeth *sura*, in fact, is often entitled *Sura al-Isra*. It begins with the reminder of the journey: "Glory be to God, who did take His servant for a journey by night" (*Sura* 17.1).

CHAPTER FIVE

ETHICAL PRINCIPLES

The Islamic tradition, based on the teachings of the Quran and the Hadith (see pp. 37–45), and as articulated by the Muslim religious scholars (*ulama*), directs Muslims to abide by the divine will, not simply as individuals but also as a community. According to the Quran, humankind was chosen by God to be his representative (*khalifa*) on Earth and, for this reason, all Muslims must bear responsibility for the creation of a just and moral social order.

The injunctions laid out in the Quran and the Hadith form the basis of what is known collectively as the Sharia, the "Islamic way." From this body of teachings derive the laws of the ideal Islamic social system. The Sharia is all-encompassing, and, to worship God, the Muslim must recognize that every realm of human activity bears religious significance.

LEFT: A young Muslim at prayer in the Masjid Raya mosque in Banda Aceh, Sumatra. Islam spread into Indonesia and Malaysia largely through the efforts of Muslim trading networks and Sufi orders.

The formal study of the Sharia is known as *fiqh*, or "jurisprudence." Those who study the Sharia, and thus articulate Islamic law, are known as *fuqaha* (singular *faqih*). The efforts of the first generations of legal scholars led to the emergence of schools, or traditions, of law known as *madhhab* (literally, "path," or "way"). Each *madhhab* represented the cumulative expression of a body of legal opinions associated with specific groups of prominent scholars. In Sunni Islam, four major schools emerged, each named after its ostensible founder: the Hanafi (after Abu Hanifa; died 767 CE); the Maliki (after Malik ibn Anas; ca. 715–795 CE); the Shafii (after Muhammad ibn Idris al-Shafii; 767–820 CE); and the Hanbali (after Ahmad ibn Hanbal; died 855 CE).

Sunni scholars discern four sources of Islamic law. First and foremost is the Quran, the direct expression of the divine will. The second authoritative source is the Hadith, the teachings of the Prophet himself. The third source is *ijma*, or "consensus," which refers to an agreed interpretation among scholars of a given legal issue. *Ijma* was an effective means of establishing conformity of opinion. *Qiyas*, or "reasoning on the basis of analogy," is the fourth source of law—it proved to be a useful tool with which scholars could reach legal decisions on issues for which the Quran and the Hadith provided no clear guidance. Shia scholars differ from their Sunni colleagues in placing greater value on the exercise of human reason and intellect. Therefore, instead of *qiyas*, the Shias have *aql* or *ijtihad*, "individual reasoning."

From early on in the development of the Islamic legal tradition, laws were divided into two categories: those that concern the relationship between humankind and God; and those that relate to the integrity of the human community. Each set of laws was divided, in turn, into five categories of human ethical conduct: "required," "recommended," "indifferent" (or "permissible"), "reprehensible," and "forbidden." In the sphere of human relationships with God, five acts of devotion (*ibadat*, singular *ibada*) are "required" practice for Muslims. These acts are often referred to as the "Five Pillars" of Islam and constitute the Islamic ritual system.

The first of the five duties is uttering the Shahada, the Islamic profession of faith: "There is no god but God, and Muhammad is His messenger."

The second—and in the opinion of many, central—duty is prayer (*salat*). This requirement is made clear in the Quran and by the Prophet himself. In one of many Hadith in which he speaks of prayer, Muhammad is quoted as saying: "When each of you performs his prayer, he is in intimate communication with his Lord."

The Quran refers to several kinds of prayer. In
Islamic law, the "required," or major, prayer consists of a
cycle of prayers performed by Muslims five times daily,
following ritual cleansing. Other forms of prayer are not
considered obligatory. The designated times for *salat* are
sunset, early evening, dawn, midday, and mid-afternoon.
Daily life in Muslim regions and neighborhoods is punc-
tuated by the call to prayer *(adhan)*, which is made by
the *muadhdhin* (often pronounced "muezzin"), usually
from the mosque "tower," or *minaret* (see p. 75).

Before prayer, whether in the mosque, at home, or
in the workplace, Muslims must prepare themselves by
focusing upon the act at hand. Physical purity is achieved
through ritual cleansing prior to each session of prayer.
The prayer cycle begins with the *takbir* (*"Allahu akhbar,"*
"God is most great") and the opening *sura* of the Quran,
al-Fatiha (see pp. 34–35). The worshiper then performs
a cycle of four physical postures—standing, bowing,
prostrating, and sitting—that are accompanied by utter-
ances, some obligatory, others voluntary. Each cycle is
called a *raka* and the number of cycles varies depending on
which of the prayers is being performed.

The third of the central Islamic duties is *zakat* or
"required almsgiving." The Quran and the Hadith speak
of it not only as an act of worship but also as the means

by which Muslims provide for one another. It is distinct from voluntary alms and traditionally has been calculated as a percentage of income, although levels of wealth, and so the ability to pay, are duly recognized.

The fourth duty is to participate in the fast (*sawm*) that takes place through Ramadan—the ninth Islamic month—which marks the onset of revelation to Muhammad. The fast applies to daylight hours, during which Muslims must refrain from eating, drinking, and smoking.

The Hajj, the pilgrimage to the sacred city of Mecca, is the fifth ritual duty. All believers are called upon to perform the Hajj at least once, but only if they are able to ensure that their dependants will be taken care of while they embark on the journey. For the Muslim, the performance of the Hajj "makes good for him in the sight of his Lord" (*Sura* 22.30).

To understand the shaping of Islamic law, it is essential to realize that Muslim legal scholars have seldom been subject to a central religious authority, as is the case, for example, in the Roman Catholic tradition. Put simply, there is no "church" in Islam. Early Islamic scholars created a body of principles and opinions that were viewed as normative. However, each generation of scholars was confronted by situations for which the existing body of opinions offered little guidance. Under these circumstances, it was the responsibility of the scholar to formulate his own conclusions. Such an opinion is known as a *fatwa* (plural *fatawa*), and is issued when the scholar is approached by someone, often a state-appointed judge (*qadi*), who is seeking guidance in a case. When an individual or a group wishes to sway public opinion on a topic deemed to be of great importance, a *fatwa* may simply be issued rather than actively sought out. A *fatwa*, however, is only an opinion and is not, therefore, legally binding. Individuals are at liberty to seek the opinion of a second scholar—which may, of course, differ from that of the first.

The term *fatwa* gained wide circulation in the West following the Ayatollah Khomeini's pronouncement, in February 1990, against the novelist Salman Rushdie. Khomeini's *fatwa* condemned Rushdie for his representation of the Prophet Muhammad in his 1988 novel, *The Satanic Verses*. The *fatwa* treated Rushdie as an apostate for whom, according to strict interpretation of Islamic law, death was the required punishment. Most commentators paid little heed to the fact that many other Muslim scholars challenged the validity of the opinion (however uncomfortable they may have been with Rushdie's views).

The Islamic tradition, then, is far from monolithic and is the product of many centuries of scholarship and internal debate. The internal debates that have shaped Islamic thought can be seen in relation to the concept of *jihad*—a term that has too often been misrepresented in the West.

The main courtyard of the madrasa *of the al-Azhar mosque in Cairo, Egypt, a principal center of Sunni legal teaching.*

In the Quran, and in the tradition, *jihad* is understood as "struggling in the name of, or in the defense of, the faith." The complex term, widely discussed in Islamic letters, has been subject to considerable interpretation and debate over the ages. However, most scholars agree that it contains an imperative for every Muslim, and for the community at large, to struggle against all that might corrupt God's word and cause disharmony.

Almost all discussions of the term emphasize the following: that *jihad* is a means by which to serve God and that an essential component of the "struggle" is internal, or spiritual, whereby the individual Muslim strives to be as good a "servant of God" as possible. The Prophet, on returning from a *jihad* (here, a military campaign), is quoted in one Hadith as saying: ". . . we have returned from the lesser *jihad* to the greater *jihad*." Two kinds of "struggle" or "war" are being referred to here. The greater, internal, struggle is in striving to resist wrongdoing ("sin"), heedlessness, and immorality—this is carried out by performing the ritual duties of Islam and by otherwise serving as an example of piety and righteousness to others (Muslims and non-Muslims alike). The second, external, struggle ("the lesser *jihad*") calls upon Muslims to act with force, indeed to wage war, when

Islam, or the Islamic community (*Umma*), is perceived to be under threat—for example, by invasion, oppressive foreign rule, or forced conversion. The Quran and the Hadith speak of the need, under such circumstances, for Muslims to take up "the sword" in defense of the faith.

Significant examples of Muslim states or groups carrying out such warfare include the campaigns organized in the twelfth century against the Crusader principalities in Palestine (especially Jerusalem) and, in the twentieth century, against British and French colonial control. Islamic scholarship has been careful to define clearly the circumstances under which war should be waged and to elucidate the rules or conditions that should be observed throughout. For example, it is stressed that women and children should not be harmed and that homes and other private properties should not be destroyed.

Some Muslims have chosen to interpret *jihad* in more militant terms. Key examples in the twentieth and twenty-first centuries are the activities of such groups as Islamic Jihad in Egypt and the Qaida network under Osama bin Laden. To their many Muslim detractors, these groups and their ideas have represented a distortion of Islamic teachings and, as a result, have been widely condemned.

Marriage in the Quran and Hadith

" It is He who created you from a single being
And of the same nature did He make his mate
So that he might incline to her... "
(*Surat al-Araf*, 7.189)

" The Prophet said: 'A woman is married for four
(reasons): for her wealth, the (reputation of) her family,
her beauty and her religiousness. Give precedence to
those who possess religiousness.' "

" The Prophet saw the women and children returning
from a wedding celebration. He arose and said:
'By God, you are the most beloved of people to me.'
He repeated it three times. "
(Hadith, from the collection of al-Bukhari)

From the Quran and Hadith (collection of al-Bukhari), translated by Matthew S. Gordon.

Commentary

Islamic law devotes considerable attention to domestic life.
Some seventy verses of the Quran treat such topics as
marriage, divorce, inheritance, and the rearing of children.
Marriage is regarded in the Islamic tradition as an essential
unit of society, that is, as vital to the integrity of the

Islamic *Umma*. This view has cultural origins but draws direct support from many indications in both the Quran and Hadith regarding the divine expectation that humans will marry and bear offspring.

In Islamic law, marriage (*nikah*) is treated as a contract between two parties, usually two families. It entails oaths of loyalty, respect, and support on the part of both partners and before God. Marriage contracts stipulate that the husband provides a dowry, which becomes the wife's private property. The contract also makes physical contact between a man and a woman morally acceptable and legal, and any attempt to render the contract void—that is, through divorce—is taken very seriously. Every attempt at reconciliation is to be sought out. Divorce can be initiated by either partner although traditional Islamic law generally makes it difficult for women to succeed. Islamic law permits men to have up to four wives, citing an explicit Quranic verse: "Marry women of your choice, two, three, or four" (*Sura* 4.3). Women can have but one husband. While it is clear that polygamy has been practiced throughout Islamic history, particularly in the Near East, its extent is impossible to measure. Modern debate often centers on a verse that is seen to negate the principle of polygamy: "You will never be able to act fairly between the women no matter how strong your desire (to do so)" (*Sura* 4.129).

CHAPTER SIX

SACRED SPACE

The unity of faith that is characteristic of the otherwise quite diverse Islamic community is expressed in physical form in the principal site of Islamic worship: the mosque (*masjid*). All mosques share the same basic plan, yet many possess secondary features that reflect their particular cultural, geographical, and historical contexts. Mosques often perform different functions from churches in the Christian tradition and, to the casual observer, may appear free of the symbols (such as the cross) that often set sacred buildings apart from others. However, calligraphy, symbolic art, and other distinctive elements appear extensively.

In addition to mosques, Islamic devotional buildings also include the tombs of the Shia Imams (see p. 57 and pp. 88–89) and shrines used to venerate local "saints" (see pp. 56–57).

LEFT: The mihrab *(prayer niche) of the Faruq mosque in the center of Khartoum, the Sudanese capital. Founded in the 11th century, the mosque has had extensive refurbishment, particularly in the mid-20th century.*

A primary function of the mosque is to provide the means by which worshipers can orient themselves toward the most sacred physical site in Islam, the Kaba in Mecca. The *mihrab* (or prayer niche)—the central architectural feature and often the most carefully decorated element of the mosque—indicates the *qibla*, the direction in which the Muslim is to pray.

The Kaba is a powerful symbol of the divine presence and is referred to in the Quran as the "House of God." The structure is believed to have been built by Adam and then rebuilt and purified by Abraham.

The environs of Mecca, and the city itself, are forbidden to non-Muslims. At the climax of the great pilgrimage, the Hajj (see pp. 85–86), the faithful circle the sacred shrine seven times and attempt to touch the black stone—seen as the physical symbol of the primordial bond linking God and humankind—that is located in one corner of the Kaba. Within the limits of Mecca, Muslims are expected to comport themselves in humble fashion. Fighting, hunting, and all forms of bloodshed are banned within the sacred confines and, in general, the city is considered to be a sanctuary.

The second function of the mosque is to provide a place for congregational prayer. Although Muslims are not required to pray in a mosque (any clean, quiet locale, including the home, can be transformed into a place of prayer), Islamic law does recommend its use. The one prayer that is normally required to take place in the mosque is the Friday midday session, and, in many areas of the Islamic world, this applies particularly to men. Women customarily pray at home—when they do use mosques, separate areas are designated for them.

Nearly all mosques include the *minaret* or "tower"— originally a quite separate building—which today is the place from which the call to prayer, the *adhan*, is usually made. A source of fresh water, such as a fountain, provides the water required for the ritual cleansing (*wudu*) that precedes each of the five sessions of daily prayer. The *dikka*, or raised platform, a later addition to mosque architecture, was traditionally used by assistants to the *imam* (in this context, the *imam* is the person who delivers the Friday sermon from the "pulpit," or *minbar*.)

The mosque is believed to have its origins in Muhammad's own house in Medina, which is said to have contained an open area for communal prayer, a covered area for protection from the elements, and some indication of the *qibla* (the direction in which to pray).

Over the course of Islamic history, builders and architects have worked with these elements in a variety of different styles and materials. The early Muslims,

during and immediately after the period of the conquests, either adapted existing structures, such as Christian churches, or constructed what were probably very
rudimentary mosques. Quite early on, the distinction
emerged between small, local mosques and larger,
congregational ones used not only for private prayer
and study but also for the Friday communal session and
weekly sermon (*khutba*). Reflecting Byzantine and

*The 12th-century Kalyan minaret in Bukhara, modern-day
Uzbekistan, was restored in the early 16th century following
damage incurred from the Mongol invasions.*

Iranian influences, new architectural features began to appear, such as the *mihrab* and the *minbar*. Among the most impressive examples of early mosques are the Umayyad mosque in Damascus, the Aqsa mosque in Jerusalem, and two built in Samarra, neither of which survives today. From a later period, Ottoman mosques are widely held to be among the finest examples of Islamic architecture. Of these structures, those designed by the great Ottoman architect Sinan (1499–1588) stand out. The finest of Sinan's mosques is perhaps the Selimiye mosque in the modern Turkish city of Edirne.

Two further structures joined the mosque as features of the pre-modern Islamic urban landscape. As the many branches of Islamic education flourished, the need arose for buildings to house students and classes. The *madrasa* (religious college) is believed to have emerged in eastern Iran by the tenth century. Hardly distinguishable from a *madrasa*, both in function and form, is the Sufi lodge, often known as a *khanqah*. It also developed in eastern Iran in the tenth and eleventh centuries as the site of Sufi instruction and practice. In time, the larger Sufi orders created networks of lodges across whole regions of the Islamic world. The celebrated Moroccan scholar and traveler Ibn Battuta (see pp. 20–21) refers to his many visits to such lodges.

Al-Muqaddasi's *The Geography of al-Muqaddasi*

❝ As regards my statement that [Jerusalem] is the most sublime of cities, it is because it joins as one this world and the next. He who is of the offspring of this world and seeks after the next world finds it in the market here; he who is of the offspring of the next world and yet whose soul draws him to the pleasure of this world will find it here. As for its delightful climate, its cold does not afflict nor does its heat cause harm. As for its excellence, nowhere can finer buildings be seen or any that are better cared for or a more beautiful mosque.... as for the eminence of the city, it is because it is to be the site of the Resurrection and, on the Day of Judgment, the place in which the risen dead will gather. Yes, it is true that Mecca and Medina are blessed with the Kaba and the Prophet but on the Day of Resurrection they will hasten together to [Jerusalem] and so it will encompass all that is sublime. ❞

From *The Geography of al-Muqaddasi*, translated by Matthew S. Gordon.

Commentary

This tribute to Jerusalem comes from the tenth-century Arab geographer al-Muqaddasi (died ca. 990 CE), himself a denizen of the city, the third holiest in Islam. Its significance to Muslims relates in particular to the sites located in the area known as the Haram al-Sharif ("The Noble Sanctuary"). The Haram is a large platform constructed in the first century BCE for the Second Jewish Temple, one surviving wall of which is considered to be the holiest site of Judaism.

Of the Haram's many sites, none is more venerated than the Dome of the Rock (*Kubbat al-Sakhra*) and the Aqsa mosque, which date to the eighth century, although both were enlarged in later periods. Islamic tradition associates the Dome of the Rock with the Prophet's Ascension (see p. 50); it is from the rock that he arose to the divine presence. A graceful structure, it is among the finest expressions of pre-modern Islamic architecture.

The Haram al-Sharif's significance to Muslims has made it a flashpoint of the Palestinian–Israeli conflict. The brief tour in September 2000 by the Israeli politician Ariel Sharon, accompanied by a force of troops and policemen, is seen by many observers as the spark for a renewed period of protest by the Palestinian populace of the Israeli-occupied West Bank and Gaza.

CHAPTER SEVEN

SACRED TIME

The Islamic year is based on a lunar calendar and is informed by a rich pattern of commemoration and devotion. The expressions of devotion fall into two broad categories. The first includes the ritual duties associated with the "Five Pillars" (see pp. 63–65), and with events such as the Prophet's birthday and the major festivals that are celebrated in conjunction with Ramadan and the Hajj. The second category consists of less regular but no less significant activities such as rites of passage, marriage celebrations, funeral rites, and festivities linked with local beliefs or revered figures.

The Shia community carries out rituals in addition to these. But in all cases, the calendar activities constitute a firm affirmation of the relationship with God and of the Muslim's commitment to Islamic communal life.

LEFT: A fountain in the arcaded courtyard of the 14th-century Attarin madrasa *in Fez, Morocco. Public spaces in such buildings often function as important centers of community life.*

The Islamic calendar consists of twelve months, the first being Muharram. A lunar calendar, it falls behind the solar calendar by approximately eleven days annually. Thus every month passes through the solar seasons in a cycle lasting around thirty-two and a half years. The establishment of the Islamic calendar is usually associated with the Caliph Umar ibn al-Khattab (reigned 634–644 CE), who is said to have ordered that the cycle of twelve lunar months begin with the day of the Hijra (see p. 13)—July 16, 622 CE.

New Year's Day celebrations are held throughout the Islamic world on the First of Muharram. The first ten days of Muharram—known as Ashura (from the Arabic for "ten")—are also significant, although in rather different ways in the Sunni and Shia traditions. In many areas of the Sunni world, the first ten days of the month are considered blessed and the tenth day is treated as a non-obligatory, or voluntary, day of fasting. Islamic sources indicate that the fast of Ashura originated in a day-long Jewish fast adapted by the early Muslims.

The Shia tradition, however, uses the ten-day period as a time of profound mourning, both for their Imams and for the community. The Ashura rituals commemorate the martyrdom of the Prophet's grandson, al-Husayn, by the troops of the Umayyad caliphate in the year 680 CE. This complex of rituals includes recitations of elegiac texts, visitations to the tombs of the Imams (see p. 88–89), and public processions. The processions often include self-flagellation by small groups of men. *Taziya*s, or dramatic reenactments of the deaths of al-Husayn and the other Imams, are also staged. These extended reenactments—which are, essentially, Passion plays—elicit highly charged responses of sorrow and grief from their audience and thus provide a moment of catharsis and redemption.

The birthday (Mawlid al-nabi) of the Prophet Muhammad is celebrated on the twelfth day of the third Islamic month (Rabia al-Awwal). Celebrations were probably low-key early in Islamic history but became more lavish under the Fatimid dynasty in Egypt and, later, under the Turkish Ottoman state. As many observers have noted, local Sufi orders played a crucial part in popularizing the event. However, these festivities have not been free of controversy: pre-modern Muslim scholars often expressed disdain for them and, in the modern period, the Wahhabi movement (see p. 89) has condemned them as a non-Islamic accretion.

An obligatory fast, one of the "Five Pillars," is observed during Ramadan, the ninth Islamic month. The fast is, quite simply, a remarkable display of

communal worship that is characterized not only by a
heightened religious sense but also by a greater emphasis upon social and family ties. The Islamic sources
associate the selection of Ramadan as the month of fast
with the revelation of the Quran: the first occasion of

*Muslim girls studying in a mosque in Bradford, England.
There has recently been renewed interest in the faith among the
offspring of Muslim immigrants to Europe and North America.*

revelation took place on the twenty-seventh day of Ramadan, an event termed Laylat al-qadr ("The Night of Power"). The Quran refers to The Night of Power as "better than a thousand months" (*Sura* 97.3).

Muslims end each day of fast with prayer and a meal, known in many areas as the *iftar*. As the many accounts of Muslims attest, the physical demands of fasting pale in significance to its spiritual and social rewards. The subdued daytime atmosphere of Islamic towns and cities is transformed with the day's end and the taking of *iftar*: streets come alive with strolling families, busy cafes, and a general sense of festiveness. The close of the fast is then celebrated in one of two great feast days of the calendar year, the Id al-Fitr ("The Feast of Fast-Breaking"), which takes place on the first of Shawwal, the tenth month. For several days, Muslims customarily gather with kin for extended meals, gift sharing, and religious devotion. The Id is a national holiday in many Muslim nations, and is thus a time to visit home and family. It is an occasion in which Muslims celebrate their faith and community, and express gratitude to God for having seen the *Umma*, and each believer, through the rigors of the fast.

The final month of the Islamic calendar is Dhu al-Hijja, the month of the pilgrimage to Mecca (see p. 65 and p. 74). All believers are obliged to perform the Hajj at least once, although Islamic law stipulates that they must be able to afford the journey while ensuring that dependants are provided for. Thus, in practice, most Muslims are unable to perform the pilgrimage but are not considered in any sense the lesser for that reason. Many Muslim states seek to provide support to would-be pilgrims—in Malaysia, for example, a national lottery offers an expenses-paid Hajj to its winners. The second of the great feast days of Islam then occurs on the tenth day of Dhu al-Hijja and is known as Id al-Adha ("The Feast of Sacrifice") or Id al-Kabir ("The Great Feast").

Rites of passage also form an important part of the Muslim calendar. The entry into life of the infant Muslim is marked by celebration and the utterance of the Fatiha and the Shahada (see p. 26 and pp. 34–35). Naming signifies religious identity and it remains common practice to take up the names of revered figures of Islamic history—thus, Muhammad, Ali, Hasan, and Husayn are all widely used. Male names also include those derived from God's own sacred names (such as Abd Allah, Abd al-Rahman). The common use of the names Khadija and Aisha for girls underscores the significance attached to the women of the Prophet's household.

Education begins informally in the home as children memorize Quranic phrases, religious songs, and the like.

Formal instruction in the Quran, the Hadith, and devotional practice take place either in classrooms or in private centers; much depends on the extent to which a given modern Islamic state permits religious instruction in state-run schools. As children learn to recite and copy down verses of the Quran, they acquire not simply the skills of reading and writing but also a close knowledge of the central teachings of their faith. Muslim scholars and teachers draw inspiration from the stress placed by the Quran and the Hadith upon the acquisition of knowledge and its dissemination.

Circumcision of Muslim boys often takes place around the age of ten or, in some areas, with the demonstration that the child has memorized the Quran. Following the brief operation, various celebrations are held to mark the entry into full Muslim life. In some Islamic societies, including Egypt and Sudan, the practice of female circumcision has generated considerable controversy. Muslim scholars diverge widely on whether or not it should be considered a requirement, and many argue against it on the grounds that it is local practice with little or no basis in Quranic law. Legal bans in certain Islamic states have not led to its disappearance.

The calendar year is also marked by rites associated with marriage as well as death and burial (see pp. 92–97).

Modern Visitation Devotions

❝ My lord, to thee is my mission, and through thee I see mediation with my Lord for the attainment of my purpose. And I bear witness that he who seeks thy mediation does not fail, and he who makes request through thee is known never to be turned away with his need unmet. ❞

❝ O Muhammad, O Abu al-Qasim, thou art my father and my mother. I beg God for thine intercession and that of the Imams born from thee.
[Prayer repeated, replacing the name of Muhammad by that of each of the twelve Imams in turn.] ❞

From *Muslim Devotions*, edited by Constance Padwick. Oneworld Publications: Oxford, 1996, p. 46

Commentary

These passages are drawn from a modern Iranian pilgrimage manual, and are representative of devotional materials used widely in the Islamic world. The excerpts voice a direct appeal by Shia worshipers to their Imams; these and similar texts have been used for centuries during visitations to the Imams' tombs. Visitations (sing. *ziyara*) are also paid by Muslims—Sunni and Shia alike—to the tombs of other venerated figures of local or regional standing. The visit to the Prophet's tomb in Medina that is often an element of the Hajj for many pilgrims is such a visitation rite.

Like the Muharram ceremonies, the practice of *ziyara* provides Shia Muslims with the opportunity to express their devotion to the Imams. The central example of *ziyara* is the visit to Imam Husayn's tomb in Karbala (today in southern Iraq). Significance of the visitation rite lies in part with the opportunity afforded the pilgrim to experience physical proximity to the venerated figure. The visit itself includes circumambulation of the tomb, recitation of Quranic verses, the donation of alms usually intended for the upkeep of the site, and prayers of the kind cited here that constitute a request to the Imam for intercession with God on behalf of the worshiper. Belief in the Imam's mediating powers is closely tied to faith; it is precisely because of their devotion that, in the Final Judgment, the Imam (usually Imam Husayn) will raise the true believers to glory.

Ziyara has drawn its measure of criticism over the centuries. The eighteenth-century Wahhabi movement in Arabia, with its strict reading of Islamic teachings, condemned the practice. Wahhabism went on to become the doctrinal foundation of Saudi Arabia, thus tomb visitation and related practices are no longer found in much of the Arabian peninsula.

CHAPTER EIGHT

DEATH AND THE AFTERLIFE

The Islamic tradition holds to the idea of an afterlife, knowledge of which may be gained through the Quran, the Hadith, and the exegetical literature. Believing in the afterlife is seen as an essential aspect of Islamic faith, because, in so doing, Muslims affirm the presence of God (the Creator, *al-Khaliq*) and the inevitability of his divine justice. It also serves to explain the significance and purpose of this life, with its manifold trials and demands: "Every soul shall taste of death and only on the Day of Judgment shall each of you receive your full recompense" (*Sura* 3.185).

The Quran treats death not so much as an ending as a return to God, the source of all things, the sole possessor of true and perfect reality. Just as God creates, so too he decrees the moment at which all things cease to be.

LEFT: A traditional Islamic funeral rite in Kashgar, a predominantly Muslim city in western China.

Death is the decision by God to end the temporary existence led by human beings on Earth. It is a shift from one mode of life to another. The earthly life is conceived of as fleeting, incomplete, and—because God alone can be perfect—inevitably flawed. Death is likewise an impermanent state: the physical body crumbles and disappears, as the soul (Arabic *nafs*), now freed of physical constraints, moves on to a different plane.

Customarily, after death, prayers are said for the deceased and the corpse is washed and prepared. Islamic law generally holds that only martyrs are to be buried as they died, without such preparation. Burial usually takes place on the morning after death. In many regions of the Islamic world, funeral processions are common, although the Hadith literature records the Prophet's disapproval of elaborate or emotionally wrought obsequies.

In one such text, the Prophet cautions women against expressing grief by rending clothing or covering their heads in dust; these may have been pre-Islamic practices. Muhammad is also said to have opposed all but the simplest of grave markers, and while there have been exceptions to this—such as the monumental tombs of the Mameluke rulers of Egypt (1250–1517 CE)—the majority of Muslim graves are plain and unadorned.

In the Quranic universe, and particularly in the workings of heaven and hell, the angels and *jinn* (see p. 25) play key roles. The angels include Gabriel (Jibril) and Izrail (or Azrail), the angel of death. The latter is one of four archangels and was chosen by God for his particular "office" because of his determination and ruthlessness. A third archangel in the Islamic cosmology is Israfil, the trumpet blower. He is said to be the one who reads the names of those judged by God prior to their departure to their designated realm. As his nickname suggests, he will rouse the dead at the appointed hour with a mighty blast of his musical instrument.

As is often pointed out in modern scholarship, the Quran devotes considerably more space to descriptions of heaven and hell than do other scriptures. The short, often intense, verses of the Meccan period contain a series of references to both abodes, thus underscoring their central theme—the inevitability of divine judgment. Hell, known by various terms, is the domain of fire, agony, and the most terrible suffering: "It is a fire burning fiercely!" (*Sura* 101.11). The descriptions of heaven or paradise depict a garden of lyrical beauty, beneath which "rivers flow; they will dwell therein forever" (*Sura* 98.9). The Quranic images of paradise continue to move Muslim poets and lyricists to compose verse on these same themes.

A central problem for Islamic theologians, as for their Jewish and Christian counterparts, is to establish a definition of free will and responsibility: on what basis are humans to be judged if God has preordained all things? Debates on this issue among early Muslim scholars reflected, in part, contemporary ideological and political divisions. Opponents of the Umayyad caliphate (see p. 15 and pp. 51–52) argued strongly for the existence of human choice and the requirement that all humans accept responsibility for their actions. However, Umayyad partisans espoused the idea of predestination, arguing that God has ordained all things beforehand, including, of course, the rule of the Umayyads. The emphasis on human free will was taken up in the ninth century CE by a group of scholars known as the Mutazilites. Their concern was to promote the idea that evil in the world could never be of divine origin but was the outcome of human behavior alone. Lengthy debate led to a certain compromise by later Sunni thinkers, among them al-Ashari (died 935 CE), who argued that God, while retaining his omnipotence, also provides humankind with a "modicum" (or, in other readings, a "brief moment") of freedom and thus responsibility.

*A depiction of an angel, from a colorfully illustrated page
of a 16th-century manuscript found in Bukhara.*

Urdu Primer on Death and Tomb Visitation

" Remember the covenant…which is the witness that there is no god but God and Muhammad is the Apostle of God…and that thou art well satisfied with God as (thy) One Lord and with Islam as (thy) religious practice and with Muhammad as Apostle and Prophet. This is the first abiding place of the abodes of the other world and the last abiding place of the abodes of this transitory world….Let them [the two angels; see p. 97] not disturb thee…for they are only creatures, a part of God's creation. And when they ask thee, 'Who is thy Lord and who is thy Prophet and what is thy *imam* [prayer leader], and thy religion, and thy *qibla* [prayer direction], and thy brethren?'. . . say, 'God is my Lord and Muhammad my Prophet, the Quran is my imam and the Kaba my *qibla*, and all the believers and Muslims are my brethren.' "

From *Muslim Devotions*, edited by Constance Padwick. Oneworld Publications: Oxford, 1996, p. 279.

Commentary

Islamic belief holds to the idea of the judgment of each individual after death, and in a final apocalyptic judgment of all souls. In the Hadith, scholarly commentaries, and popular religious literature, the fate of the individual takes place in several phases. At first, the body ceases to function, thereby releasing the soul, which undergoes an examination by angels. Exegetical and popular text—such as the Urdu primer from which this piece is extracted—name two angels as the ones responsible for the "interrogation," Munkar and Nakir, although neither name appears in the Quran. From this point, the soul occupies the grave until the world ends and all humankind is resurrected from the dead to face the final Day of Judgment. God will judge humans—in one popular image, he employs a set of scales—according to their response to the prophetic message delivered by Muhammad and the earlier prophets. This response is understood largely in terms of obedience to the divine will: the unbeliever rejects the conduct codified in the Quran and Hadith and thus earns a place in hell, while the true believer—the *mumin*—whose life conformed to the Prophetic example (*Sunna*), is brought into paradise.

CHAPTER NINE

SOCIETY AND RELIGION

Issues that confront the contemporary Islamic world are rooted in both the recent and distant past. Responses to such issues reflect the disparate ways in which Muslims, both within and between states, interpret Islam's teachings—thus, on any given issue, reactions will range from sharply secular to militantly religious.

In no sense, therefore, can the Islamic world be considered monolithic. Equally significant is the fact that questions that are unique to Islam jostle with problems of the modern period in general—for example, the expansion of new technologies, the impact of post–Cold War realities, the spread of Western popular culture, and the transformation of world economic practices. While Muslims may share a religion, they are also citizens of nation states that have their own developmental problems.

LEFT: Palestinian women in traditional dress at prayer outside the Dome of the Rock in Jerusalem during the month of Ramadan—a period of heightened devotion throughout the Islamic world.

Islam flourishes today not simply in areas that have long contained majority Muslim populations, such as North Africa and the Middle East. Indonesia and Malaysia are among the largest Islamic nations, and both states play significant roles in the Islamic world—for example, in the Organization of the Islamic Conference (OIC). The emergence in the 1990s of the new Central Asian states, among them Kazakhstan and Uzbekistan, signaled the onset of new political and religious dynamics in the region, particularly in relation to Turkey, Russia, and China.

No less apparent is the growth of the Muslim populations of Europe and North America, with their complex mix of immigrants and native converts. Islam has flourished within the African American population: Chicago, New York, and other cities are home to some two to three million African American Muslims. The largest number are Sunni Muslims, many from families that earlier belonged to the Nation of Islam, the first formal Islamic movement in North America. These populations face a number of questions as a result of their minority standing. For example, how does adherence to Islamic codes—particularly with regard to personal-status law (marriage, divorce, inheritance, and child custody)—relate to civil law?

The status of Sharia law (see pp. 65–66) is among the many complex issues confronting the Islamic world. Several Islamic states introduced Western-style legal codes immediately upon their emergence from colonialism. Islamic revivalism, coupled with disenchantment with the orientation of these states, fueled an insistence that legal codes be overhauled and replaced with Islamic codes. Central to the debate, however, has also been a call for the reform of Sharia law—that is, a desire for the creation of regulations that are more in tune with contemporary needs.

The debates over religion, law, and society within the modern Islamic world reflect a complex mix of historical processes. One such process concerns relations with the West and the legacy of colonialism. By the early twentieth century, most of the Islamic world had fallen under the control of Britain, France, and other Western powers. Imperialism often exacted a grim toll upon local economic structures and social cohesion.

The nation states that emerged from under colonial domination were often led by Western-oriented elites who created secular, centralized regimes bent on establishing modern and economically vital states. The results usually fell short of the mark; as the flush of independence faded, regimes resisted economic innovation and political liberalization, and, in response to criticism, usually turned to political repression as well as reliance upon either the United States or the Soviet Union. The result was often a yawning divide between ruling elites and their citizenries—a crisis exacerbated by decades-long government waste and corruption coupled with growing levels of poverty.

To many, a perceived fragmentation of the Islamic world was related to the abandonment of Sharia law. A broad movement of reformist Islamic thought emerged by the early twentieth century to offer a variety of responses as to the future of the Islamic *Umma*. The reformist leadership included such figures as Jamal al-Din al-Afghani (1839–1897), Sayyid Ahmad Khan (1817–1898), Rashid Rida (1865–1935), Muhammad Abduh (1849–1905), and Abd al-Hamid ben Badis (died 1940). Many shared the conviction that revitalized Islamic principles were the necessary route to modern, forward-looking Muslim societies.

Political unease and economic stagnation, along with the persistent crises in Palestine, Kashmir, Chechniya, and the Sudan have only fueled a growing sense of tension throughout the Islamic world. Developments in at least three areas moved much of the debate away from reform toward Islamic revivalism and even revolution.

In Iran, developments in the nineteenth century, particularly the decline of the Qajar dynasty (1794–1925), strengthened the "Twelver" Shia *ulama*. This set the stage for tensions in the twentieth century between the Iranian monarchy and a militant Islamist movement that, ultimately, emerged under the spiritual leadership of Ayatollah Khomeini. The success of the 1979 Islamic Revolution brought Khomeini to power in Iran. In India, the ideas of Abu Ala Mawdudi (1903–1979) led to the creation in the 1940s of the Jamaat-i-Islami and its offshoots in modern Pakistan. In Egypt, the activism of Hasan al-Banna (1906–1949) prepared the ground for the emergence of the Muslim Brotherhood. Subsequent decades led to the creation of newer organizations such as Hamas in Palestine and Hizballah in Lebanon.

A common refrain from such movements was that "Islam is [or provides] the solution." However, the phrase does not imply that these groups seek a return to some idealized Islamic past, or are a throwback to "medieval" patterns. On the contrary, and despite frequent references to the achievements of Islamic history, they tend to present a modern vision of Islamic society. Many observers point out that the militant application of Islamic vocabulary and symbols—be it the veil or the Quran itself—has little precedent in the Islamic past.

Reinterpreting the Quran from a Modern Woman's Perspective

❝ I believe the Quran adapts to the context of the modern woman as smoothly as it adapted to the original Muslim community fourteen centuries ago. This adaptation can be demonstrated if the text is interpreted with her in mind, thus indicating the universality of the text. Any interpretations which narrowly apply the Quranic guidelines only to literal mimics of the original community do an injustice to the text. No community will ever be exactly like another. Therefore, no community can be a duplicate of that original community. The Quran never states this as a goal. ❞

From *Qur'an and Women: Reinterpreting The Sacred Texts from a Woman's Perspective*, by Amina Wadud. Oxford University Press: Oxford, 1999, p. 95.

Commentary

The Islamic world has seen renewed interest in religion by younger Muslims. Symbolic of this trend is the widespread use of the *hijab* or head covering by women. Some express interest in the ideas of Islamic reform, a stance that often meets with opposition from traditionalist circles, and perhaps no issue has sparked more debate than the status of women. Veiling, gender segregation, access to higher education, and the reform of personal-status law codes are all controversial topics. The harsh measures first adopted in the 1990s by Afghanistan's radical Taliban movement—strict veiling, denial of employment to women, closure of girls' schools—underscore, in the minds of many reformers, how high the stakes are.

Arguments often center on laws to do with marriage and divorce. Sharp disagreement over the necessity to reform Islamic law in these areas often pits members of the scholarly community against those who seek, as they understand it, to develop a modern legal code that would better reflect the needs of Islamic society. A frequently cited view among reformers is that Islamic tradition has always provided for reinterpretation of the law in order to meet contemporary needs. A related argument holds that the Quran and Hadith should be read less for specific rules than for ethical principles that would provide guidance to legal specialists as they crafted new and more relevant regulations.

Closely related to the debate over reform of Islamic law is the argument over the contribution of Western feminist ideas. Significant voices urge the creation of an "Islamic feminism" that would respond to the traditions and needs of Muslim women first, thus recognizing that Western ideas of reform may not always be relevant.

GLOSSARY

adhan The call to prayer made by the *muadhdhin* (muezzin) five times daily.

Allah "The [one and unique] god" (*al-ilah*), the Creator and Judge of humankind.

aya "Sign" (of God's justice and mercy); verse of the Quran.

fatwa Juridical opinion with no binding force.

fiqh Islamic religious law.

Hadith "Report"; an account, or the body of accounts, recording the *Sunna* of Muhammad, that is, his words, teachings, and deeds.

Hajj Pilgrimage to Mecca; one of the "Five Pillars" of Islam.

ibada Act of worship; ritual duty for Muslims.

imam "Leader"; the person who leads Friday prayers—as a proper noun, Imam refers to someone regarded in Shiism as the only legitimate successor to Muhammad as a leader of the Islamic *Umma* (community).

iman Faith, belief; a central organizing principle of Islam.

Islam The act of submission to God's will; the religious tradition of Islam.

Isra Muhammad's miraculous journey from Mecca to Jerusalem on the winged Buraq.

jihad "Striving" or "struggle" to serve God; holy war.

madrasa Religious or theological school; traditionally the site in which the *ulama* was trained in Islamic law and doctrine.

masjid "Place of prostration"; mosque.

mihrab Niche in a mosque wall marking the direction of Mecca.

Miraj "Ascension," especially the Ascension of the Prophet Muhammad.

nubuwwa Prophecy, a key principle of Islamic belief.

salat Prayer; one of the "Five Pillars" of Islam.

Shahada The Islamic profession of faith ("there is no god but God and Muhammad is His messenger").

Sharia The divine will as expressed in the Quran and Hadith; Islamic sacred law.

Sunna "Path or way." Refers to the example of the Prophet, his deeds and teachings; see Hadith.

sura A section or "chapter" of the Quran.

FOR MORE INFORMATION

Islamic Assembly of North America (IANA)
PMB # 270
3588 Plymouth Road
Ann Arbor, MI 48105
Web site: http://www.iananet.org
An organization that unifies many Muslim groups to promote cooperation, education, and activism within the North American Muslim community.

The Islamic Center of America
19500 Ford Road
Dearborn, MI 48128
(313) 593-0000

Web site: http://www.icofa.com/index.html
The Islamic Center of America has been dedicated to the education of the general public and
the spiritual growth and betterment of its community. The Islamic Center has a rich history
of education and community leadership, sharing its faith and house of worship with all those
who are interested in learning about Islam.

Islamic Institute of Toronto
1630 Neilson Road
Scarborough, ON, Canada M1X 1S3
(416) 335-9173
Web site: http://www.islam.ca
A nonprofit educational institute seeking to educate Muslim and non-Muslim Canadians
about Islam.

Islamic Society of North America (ISNA)
P.O. Box 38
Plainfield, IN 46168
(317) 839-8157
Web site: http://www.isna.net
An organization that seeks to educate North American Muslims and promote cooperation
with other faiths and peoples.

Muslim Public Affairs Council (MPAC)
3010 Wilshire Boulevard, # 217
Los Angeles, CA 90010
(213) 383-3443
Web site: http://www.mpac.org
MPAC works to help American Muslims with issues of civil rights, integration, and political
representation.

The Prince Alwaleed Center for Muslim-Christian Understanding
Georgetown University
ICC 260 3700 O Street, NW
Washington, DC 20057
(202) 687-8375
Web site: http://cmcu.georgetown.edu
This Georgetown University center of learning specializes in Muslim and Muslim-
Christian issues and initiatives.

Web Sites

Due to the changing nature of Internet links, Rosen Publishing has developed an online
list of Web sites related to the subject of this book. This site is updated regularly. Please
use this link to access this list:

http://www.rosenlinks.com/rel/islam

FOR FURTHER READING

Baines, Fran, ed. *Islam* (Eyewitness Books). New York, NY: DK Publishing, 2005.

Barnes, Trevor. *Islam: Worship, Festivals, and Ceremonies from Around the World*. New York, NY: Kingfisher Publishing, 2005.

Corzine, Phyllis. *World History Series—The Islamic Empire*. Chicago, IL: Lucent Books, 2004.

Demi. *Muhammad*. New York, NY: Margaret K. McElderry Books, 2003.

Ganeri, Anita. *Muslim Festivals Throughout the Year* (A Year of Festivals Series). Mankato, MN: Smart Apple Media, 2003.

Gordon, Matthew S. *The Rise of Islam*. Westport, CT: Greenwood Press, 2005.

Hafiz, Dilara, Imran Hafiz, and Yasmine Hafiz. *The American Muslim Teenager's Handbook*. Phoenix, AZ: Acacia Publishing, 2007.

Ibrahim, Muhammad, and Anita Ganeri. *Muslim Prayer and Worship*. North Mankato, MN: Sea to Sea Publications, 2008.

Kennedy, Hugh. *When Baghdad Ruled the Muslim World*. New York, NY: Da Capo Press, 2004.

Khan, Hena. *The Night of the Moon: A Muslim Holiday Story*. San Francisco, CA: Chronicle Books, 2008.

Lindsay, James E. *Daily Life in the Medieval Islamic World*. Westport, CT: Greenwood Press, 2005.

Lombard, Maurice. *The Golden Age of Islam*. Princeton, NJ: Markus Wiener Publishers, 2003.

Macaulay, David. *Mosque*. New York, NY: Walter Lorraine Books/Houghton Mifflin Company, 2003.

Moezzi, Melody. *War on Error: Real Stories of American Muslims*. Fayetteville, AK: University of Arkansas Press, 2007.

Morris, Neil. *The Atlas of Islam: People, Daily Life and Traditions*. Hauppage, NY: Barron's Educational Series, 2003.

Young, Mitchell, ed. *Religions and Religious Movements: Islam*. Farmington Hills, MI: Greenhaven Press, 2005.

GENERAL BIBLIOGRAPHY

Abbott, Nabia. *Aishah, The Beloved of Muhammad*. New York, NY: Arno, 1973 (orig. 1942).

al-Ghazali, Abu Hamid Muhammad. *The Alchemy of Happiness*. (Trans. Claud Field; revised by Elton L. Daniel). London, England: M.E. Sharpe, 1991.

Ali, A. Yusuf. *The Koran: Translation and Commentary*. Washington, DC: American International Printing, 1946.

Ali, Muhammad. *A Manual of Hadith*. London, England: Curzon, 1977.

Arberry, A.J. *The Koran Interpreted*. New York, NY: Macmillan, 1955.

Armstrong, Karen. *Muhammad: A Biography of the Prophet*. San Francisco, CA: Harper, 1992.

Denny, F. M. *An Introduction to Islam*. New York, NY: Macmillan, 1985.

Dunn, Ross. *The Adventures of Ibn Battuta: A Muslim Traveler of the Fourteenth Century*. Berkeley, CA: University of California Press, 1986.

Ernst, C. W. *The Shambhala Guide to Sufism*. Boston, MA: Shambhala, 1997.

Esposito, John L. *The Oxford Encyclopedia of the Modern Islamic World*. 4 vols. New York, NY: Oxford University Press, 1995.

Esposito, John L. *Islam: The Straight Path*. 3rd ed. New York, NY: Oxford University Press, 1998.

Fernea, Elizabeth. *In Search of Islamic Feminism: One Woman's Global Journey.* New York, NY: Doubleday, 1998.

Gibb, H.A.R., trans. and ed. *Ibn Battuta: Travels in Asia and Africa 1325–1354.* London, England: Routledge & Kegan Paul Ltd, 1957.

Guillaume, A. *The Life of Muhammad: A Translation of Ibn Ishaq's Sirat Rasul Allah.* London, England: Oxford University Press, 1967.

Khomeini, Ruhollah. *Islam and Revolution: Writings and Declarations of Imam Khomeini.* (Trans. Hamid Algar.) Berkeley, CA: Mizan, 1987.

Momen, Moojan. *An Introduction to Shi'i Islam.* New Haven, CT: Yale University Press, 1985.

Renard, John. *Seven Doors to Islam: Spirituality and the Religious Life of Muslims.* Berkeley, CA: University of California Press, 1996.

Renard, John., ed. *Windows on the House of Islam.* Berkeley, CA: University of California Press, 1998.

Robinson, Francis. *Atlas of the Islamic World since 1500.* New York, NY: Facts On File, 1982.

Sullivan, Lawrence E., ed. *Enchanting Powers: Music in the World's Religions.* Cambridge, MA: Harvard University Press, 1997.

Wach, Joachim. (ed. J.M. Kitagawa.) *The Comparative Study of Religion.* New York, NY: Columbia University Press, 1961.

INDEX

ABOUT THE AUTHOR

Matthew S. Gordon is an Associate Professor of Islamic History at Miami University. He is the author of *The Breaking of a Thousand Swords* and *The Rise of Islam*.

ACKNOWLEDGMENTS AND PICTURE CREDITS

Unless cited otherwise here, text extracts are out of copyright or the product of the author's own translation. The following sources have kindly given their permission.

Origins and Historical Development, p. 20: *Ibn Battuta: Travels in Asia and Africa 1325–1354*. Translated and selected by H.A.R. Gibb. Routledge & Kegan Paul Ltd: London, 1957, pp. 47–48.

Sacred Persons, p. 58: from *Windows on the House of Islam*, edited by John Renard. University of California Press: Berkeley, 1998, p. 124.

Sacred Time, p. 88 and **Death and the Afterlife, p. 96:** from *Muslim Devotions*, edited by Constance Padwick. Oneworld Publications: Oxford, 1996, p. 46 and p. 279.

Society and Religion, p. 104: from *Qur'an and Women: Reinterpreting The Sacred Texts from a Woman's Perspective*, by Amina Wadud. Oxford University Press: Oxford, 1999, p. 95.

The publisher would like to thank the following people, museums, and photographic libraries for permission to reproduce their material. Every care has been taken to trace copyright holders. However, if we have omitted anyone we apologize, and will, if informed, make corrections in any future edition.

Cover, pp, 1, 3 (left) © www.istockphoto. com/Serdar Yagci; (top center) © www. istockphoto.com/Aidar Ayazbayev; (right) © www.istockphoto.com/Nicholas Belton; cover, p. 1 (top left) © www.istockphoto. com/Tjui Tjioe; (top right) © www. istockphoto.com/Alija; cover (bottom) © www.istockphoto.com/Naheed Choudhry; cover, back cover (background) © www. istockphoto.com/Thaddeus Robertson.

Page 2 Robert Harding, London; **7** Christie's Images, London; **10** Bruno Barbey/ Magnum Photos, London; **16** Stone, London; **22** Abbas/Magnum Photos, London; **28** Christie's Images, London; **36** Abbas/ Magnum Photos, London; **39** Musée Condé, Chantilly/ Bridgeman Art Library, London; **46** British Library, London/Art Archive, London; **54–55** Christie's Images, London; **60** Abbas/Magnum Photos, London; **67** James Morris/ Axiom, London; **72** Peter Sanders Photography, Chesham; **76** Cee Weston-Baker, London; **80** Peter Sanders Photography, Chesham; **84** Abbas/ Magnum Photos, London; **90** Abbas/Magnum Photos, London; **95** British Museum, London; **98** Richard T. Nowitz/ Corbis Images, London.